THE URBANA FREE LIBRARY

W9-BDV-478

DISCARDED BY THE
URBANA FREE LIBRARY

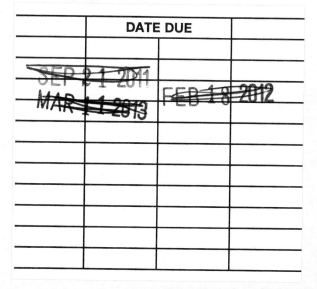

		DATE DUE	
	SEP 2 1 2011		
MAR 1 1 2013		FEB 18 2012	

THE URBANA FREE LIBRARY

TO RENEW MATERIALS CALL
(217) 367-4057

The Three Muslim Festivals

Written by Aminah Ibrahim Ali
Illustrated by Aldin Hadzic

IQRA'
International Educational Foundation
Chicago

URBANA FREE LIBRARY

10-09 Culture for Kids 17⁰⁰

Part of a Comprehensive and Systematic Program of Islamic Studies

An enrichment Book of
Islamic Manners & Traditions
Elementary Level

The Three Muslim Festivals

Chief Program Editors
Dr. Abidullah al-Ansari Ghazi
Ph.D., Comparative Religions
Harvard University

Dr.Tasneema Khatoon Ghazi
Ph.D., Curriculum Instruction
University of Minnesota

Language Editing
Huda Quraishi-Ahmed
B.Sc., University of Illinois, Chicago

Carolyn G. Baugh
B.A., Duke University

Heidi Liddle-Bhutt
M.A., University of Arkansas

Designer
Kathryn Heimberger
American Academy of Art

Illustrator
Aldin Hadzic
Sarajevo Academy of Art

Typesetting:
Sabeehuddin Khaja

Copyright © May 1998, IQRA' International
Educational Foundation
All Rights Reserved

Third Printing February, 2006
Printed in China

Special note on copyright:
This book is a part of IQRA's comprehensive
and systematic program of Islamic studies
being developed for Islamic Education.

No part of this book may be reproduced
by any means including photocopying,
electronic, mechanical, recording, or otherwise
without the written consent of the publisher.
In specific cases, permission is granted on
written request to publish or translate
IQRA's works. For information regarding
permission, write to:

IQRA' International Educational Foundation
7450 Skokie Blvd., Skokie, IL 60077
Tel: 847-673-4072, Fax: 847-673-4095
Website: www.iqra.org
Email: iqra@iqra.org

Library of Congress Catalog card Number 98-71812
ISBN 1-56316-308-X

IQRA´s Note

As the Muslim population continues to grow throughout the world, particularly in North America, we see a growing interest in Islamic traditions and culture. For this reason IQRA´ International Educational Foundation has devised a program of children´s enrichment literature to educate both Muslim and non-Muslim youth in the values and traditions of Islam. While the lessons in these books are specific to Islam, you will find that they are universal to nearly all religions. We have included a glossary to help with the Islamic terminology.

The Three Muslim Festivals is a charming collection of stories highlighting the three major celebrations of Islam: *Ramadan*, *Id al-Fitr*, and *Id al-Adha* respectively. While most children may have probably heard the names of these holidays, they may not be aware of the traditions and practices tied to each festival.

Ramadan is the ninth month of the Islamic lunar calendar during which Muslim fast from dawn to sunset. During the fast, Muslims focus on spiritual cleansing and behavior. Getting up early before dawn for *Suhur* (morning meal) and breaking the fast at sunset are times of rejoicing and contemplation for Muslim families. Neighborhood mosques provide food and drinks for the community breakfasts throughout *Ramadan*, brining together Muslims from all walks of life. Every night, there is extended night prayer during which a portion of Qur´an is recited until the Qur´an is completed, which is another festive hallmark of *Ramadan*. *Ramadan* is also charactized by a heightened sense of charity, involving both spiritual and material sacrifice.

The end of *Ramadan* is marked by the celebration of *Id al-Fitr*. The day begins with a special breakfast, the giving of *Sadaqah al-Fitr* (required charity) and congregational prayer, in the spirit of unity that is the focus of *Id*, a special effort is made to have the entire community congregate for prayer at a central place. Donning their best attire, Muslims visit each other, exchange gifts and rejoice as a community.

Id al-Adha is celebrated on the tenth of *Dhu al-Hajjah,* which is the twelfth month of the Islamic calendar. In coincides with the *Hajj* (the pilgrimage to the Kab'ah, the house of God in Makkah) and commemorates Prophet Ibrahim's (Abraham) sacrifice of his son, Isma'il (Ishmael) and his redemption by a lamb. It is a day of special thanksgiving prayers and sacrifice of a lamb, goat, or a share in a camel or a cow. The meat is distributed equally among needy, relatives or friends, and one's own family.

Certain themes are common to all Muslim festivals: prayer, charity, sharing, social interaction, and celebration without the prevalence of extravagance or commercialism. In this book, Rabiah, Musa, and Ahmad, the three main characters in the stories, take readers into their homes to witness each of their families' holiday preparations. Their stories bring to life the meaning and personal significance of these traditions. Aminah Ibrahim Ali has presented these stories in a sensitive, engaging manner, sure to appeal to both Muslims and non-Muslims alike.

Ramadan

The sound of the door closing echoed through the house. Rabiah ran to the front hall. "Did they see it yet? Did they see the moon?" she asked, breathless with excitement.

Dr. Saddiq placed her briefcase on the floor and folded Rabiah into a warm hug. "Yes, darling. I heard the news at work. *Ramadan* has started. *Ramadan Mubarak*."

Rabiah nestled into her mother's embrace, smiling to herself. The new moon always meant the beginning of a new month in the Islamic year. Yet, this month was the most special month of them all. *Ramadan*, the holiest month of the year for Muslims, had begun at last. It was a time to gather with friends and family, a time of many blessings.

Her brother Yunus appeared. "What happened?" he asked. "*Ramadan Mubarak*!" shouted Rabiah. He smiled at his sister. "Happy *Ramadan* to you too." Their mother sent them into the kitchen to start dinner preparations while she changed her clothes.

Soon, however, they heard their father's key in the door. Rabiah rushed to tell him the news. "Daddy, the new moon appeared. Tomorrow we'll begin fasting from dawn 'til sunset!"

Her father smiled broadly. "Is that a fact?" he asked, lifting Rabiah onto his broad shoulders. "We'd better take a look at this new moon ourselves."

They walked outside, with Rabiah perched on her father's shoulders and Yunus trailing behind to peer into the star-washed night. The sound of singing crickets greeted them. The moon cut a gleaming crescent in the sky.

"*Ramadan Mubarak*," said their father. "Now we'd better get inside and eat or we'll be late for the *Tarawih* prayers."

Rabiah didn't remember what *Tarawih* prayers might be, so she leaned close to her father's ear and whispered, "What are they?"

Mr. Saddiq smiled and replied, "*Tarawih* is the special prayer that we say after the nighttime prayer all through *Ramadan*. Don't forget that throughout *Ramadan* the Egyptian *Qari'* will be reciting the whole Qur'an. He will do so during the *Tarawih* prayers."

"Oh…" said Rabiah. She sighed happily as the evening breeze rushed her cheek. "It's so beautiful," she murmured, taking a last look at the shimmering moon before it faded into the inky night.

A soft kiss on her forehead roused Rabiah from her dreaming. She blinked her sleep-heavy eyes, peering into the darkness of her room, confused.

"Time for *Suhur*, honey," whispered her mother, smoothing Rabiah's tousled hair.

Then she remembered...*Ramadan*. *Suhur* was the meal they ate before beginning the fast at dawn. She slipped quickly from between her bed sheets and made her way into the brightly lit kitchen. Yunus was already at the table crunching on a slice of toast. The table was piled high with all their favorites: pancakes, eggs, cocoa. She took her seat excitedly and began to load her plate.

"We have only twenty minutes more," their father announced. He joined them at the table, a gentle smile playing across his lips as he watched his children eating.

When dawn broke, the family stated their intentions to fast:

Wa bi Sawmi ghadin nawaitu min shahri Ramadan

"O Allah, I intend to fast tomorrow during this month of *Ramadan*."

Then they prayed the dawn prayer together and all went back to their rooms to sleep for awhile before the start of the day.

Rabiah awoke later to a room flooded with sunlight. Outside her window, birds chirped as they flitted from one branch of the maple tree to another. After washing her face and brushing her teeth carefully, so as not to swallow any water-she found her mother on the back porch. The Holy Qur'an was spread across her mother's lap, its thin pages adorned with beautiful Arabic script.

Rabiah sat close to her mother on the porch swing, listening to her sweet voice reciting the sacred words. Even the singing birds seemed to pause for a moment to listen as her mother read.

When she had finished the verse, Mother pointed to a line and helped sound out the words as Rabiah read.

"That's wonderful, Rabiah," she said, kissing her on the check. "You're getting better every day. On the Day of Judgment, fasting and reading the Qur'an like this will make Allah pleased with you."

Rabiah knew that making Allah happy was the very best thing she could do. She quickly started to read another line of the Qur'an, so that Allah would be even happier with her. Just as she was finishing, she heard her brother calling from their tree-house high in the oak tree.

"Come on, Rabiah!"

She looked at her mother questioningly. Mother nodded, saying, "That's enough for today. I'll see you when I get home from work. Do everything your brother says, alright?"

"Yes Mother," she replied, and with that she jumped down off the porch and raced across the yard to where the tree stood tall and sturdy. She climbed up the ladder and soon was lost with Yunus in their tree-top world of imagination.

It wasn't until much later, when the mid-day sun was high in the sky, that she made her way back to the house. She felt a bit dizzy, and her stomach was cramping with hunger pains.

Yunus looped his arm around her shoulders. "How about some lunch?" he asked.

Rabiah looked up shyly.

"You aren't old enough to fast all day," he explained. "Young children and old people are excused from fasting; sick people and travelers too. Although, the sick and the traveler must make up for the fasting days they missed."

He walked into the kitchen and began spreading peanut butter and jelly on two thick slices of bread.

Rabiah ate and drank quietly. She had been so thirsty, and the food tasted so good, but she didn't want much. She really wanted to fast like the others. She was determined to try to do it for at least one day.

16

When her Mother
returned from her clinic,
Rabiah rushed to help her
mother in the kitchen.
There were special dishes
to prepare for *Ramadan*.
Everything smelled and
looked so good. She was
amazed that her mother
looked so calm and peaceful
after having worked and
fasted all day. Dr. Saddiq
was humming softly to herself and murmuring quiet
prayers as she prepared
each delicious dish.

At sunset, the family gathered together along with some friends and relatives. The setting sun turned the sky a brilliant copper before slipping beneath the horizon line. As Yunus made the call to prayer, their father passed out sweet dates. They all recited together:

Allahumma inni laka sumtu wa ´ala rizqi ka aftar-tu

"O Allah, for Your sake we have fasted and we break the fast with food that comes from You."

The dates and many glasses of water and fresh juices vanished as the family broke their fasts. It was time for the *Maghrib Salah*, the sundown prayer.

After praying, they gathered around the table to feast on the wonderful dishes Mother had prepared.

Their father asked them, "What did you learn from fasting today?"

Yunus straightened in his chair and took on a serious expression. "I learned how lucky I am to have food every day. There are lots of children who are hungry like I was today, all the time!"

Rabiah listened to her brother. She remembered how she had eaten at noon and wondered what it would have been like if Yunus had told her there was no food at all. She thanked Allah from the bottom of her heart for all His kind blessings.

After dinner, they piled into the car to go to the mosque. Her friends clustered around her when she arrived.

"I fasted all day," Sarah exclaimed.

Rabiah hugged her friend. "That's great!" Then she murmured, "I kept half the day."

Hibah joined them. "I fasted all day," she said, but then admitted, "But I had a glass of milk in between."

Rabiah watched as people milled around, greeting each other with *"Assalam alaikum,"* (Peace be upon you.) She saw Indians and Arabs, Indonesians and Pakistanis, whites and African-Americans, all greeting each other with warm hugs or handshakes. There were also people from South America and the Caribbean Islands, Britain and Africa, all smiling at each other. Peace really did fill the room.

Rabiah remembered her father's words: "In Islam, we are all one family. All of us are brothers and sisters; all of us are equal."

After the *Tarawih* prayers, they all sat together listening to the *Imam*.

"*Ramadan* is a month of blessings!" said the leader. "Allah has promised to reward us extra for every good deed we do in *Ramadan*. The doors of Heaven are opened during this month, and the doors of Hell are closed."

Rabiah hung on the *Imam*'s every word. She wished she could see the doors of heaven. "They must be very beautiful," she thought.

At *Suhur* the next morning, Dad told them, "Our Prophet Muhammad, (Allah's peace and blessings be upon him) said, 'Eat *Suhur* for it is a blessed nourishment.'"

Rabiah chewed sleepily on her toast. "What about poor people?" she asked. "How can they eat *Suhur*?"

"There is blessing in drinking even a sip of water," Dad answered, patting her head. Then he added, "It's the duty of those who can afford it to help the poor all over the world."

Rabiah hurt for anyone who didn't have food to eat, especially for *Suhur*. All day, Rabiah thought hard. What could she do to help the poor? It was her mother who solved her problem.

"The Women's Group will be hosting an *Iftar* for the community next Saturday-and we'll be collecting funds to provide regular *Iftars* at the mosque," she said as she pulled a steaming dish from the oven. She looked closely at Rabiah. "Do you want to help us?"

Rabiah's eyes widened. "Can I?!" When her mother nodded, Rabiah threw her arms around her, crying, "What can I do? When can I start?"

Everyone got busy raising funds that week. Rabiah helped ice cakes for the bake sale. She counted out heaps of dollar bills and coins. Now there would be enough to buy food for the *Iftar*.

On Saturday evening, she poured tall glasses of fruit juice and passed around napkins. The Women's Group had prepared tasty meats, breads, and rice. People crowded into the center. Some of the older girls and boys served the food and made sure that everyone had enough to eat.

At the end of the evening, Rabiah fell into a chair, her feet aching. Mom's cheeks dimpled as she looked proudly at her daughter. Prophet Muhammad (Peace be upon him) said that "If you provide a fasting person with food or water to break the fast, he (she) would have the same reward of that fasting person him/herself."

After that, Rabiah's feet didn't ache quite so badly. (At-Tirmidhi, Ibn Mājah)

23

The end of summer was nearing, and only ten days of *Ramadan* remained. It had been a month of joy - so many guests had filled their house with laughter, so many wonderful meals had been shared in the mosque, so many evenings had been spent visiting friends and family until late into the night.

Yunus and Rabiah were outside late one afternoon watering the yard. Glistening wet grass poked up between their bare toes. The swell of singing crickets rose up into the muggy air.

From the kitchen, Rabiah could hear the welcome clanging of pots and pans. Her stomach growled its emptiness, but she was used to it.

"Since *Suhur*, I had only one glass of milk," she said.

"By *Lailat al-Qadar* you might be fasting the whole day," Yunus replied.

"By when?" Rabiah asked. She bent to touch the gauzy orchids.

"*Lailat al-Qadar* means the Night of Power," Yunus explained. "The Qur'an says it is better than one thousand months."

"When is it?" Rabiah wanted to know.

"Prophet Muhammad (Peace be upon him) said we can expect it during the last ten nights of *Ramadan*.

Yunus turned off the water and they watched as the last drops dripped reluctantly from the nozzle. "It's a night for extra prayer. The angels come to earth and give special blessings to those who are praying. Plus, the Qur'an was first sent down on that night.

Mother called to them from the kitchen window. The sun was near to setting. Yunus dropped the hose and the two of them raced into the house.

Before the door could close, Rabiah had flown into her mother's arms. "Guess what, Mama, guess what? You'll never guess!"

Her mother looked down at her fondly. "Well, if I'll never guess, I suppose you had better tell me straight away."

Rabiah beamed with pride. "I fasted the whole day. The whole day! Not a glass of milk-not anything. And I'm not even hungry!!"

Dr. Saddiq smiled proudly. "*Ma sha Allah*! I knew you could do it." She kissed Rabiah's cheek. "What a big girl you are!"

Her father entered, carrying a newspaper. "What's all the commotion?"

"Daddy, I've fasted all day today. And I'm not even hungry, honest!"

"The whole day?" He raised his eyebrows.

Rabiah nodded earnestly.

"You know, tonight just might be *Lailat al-Qadar*, too, so that makes it extra special."

Rabiah nodded again. "I know, Yunus told me all about it."

Everyone had arranged to spend the twenty-seventh night of *Ramadan* at the Islamic Center. There was going to be *Iftar* at sundown and then *Suhur* the next morning for everyone. The *Qari'*, the special reciter of the Holy Book, would be completing the reading of the Qur'an that night.

Rabiah's heart banged hard in her chest. She hoped this was the Night of Power.

"*Id al-Fitr* is only three days away," Sarah whispered as the *adhan* was called. Rabiah looked at her friend, surprised. How could she have forgotten all about the happiest day in the whole year?

In her *Tarawih* prayers, she thanked Allah for giving her the strength to fast- even if just for the last few days. She thanked Him for a peaceful *Ramadan*, and prayed that *Id al-Fitr* would be as joy-filled as the year before. But as she looked around the *masjid* filled with so many different people, all her brothers and sisters felt suddenly sad. The coming of *Id al-Fitr* meant that *Ramadan* was ending.

28

She would miss the blessed month where everyone tried not only to fast but to be kind and generous to each other.

She would miss all the happy gatherings for *Iftar* at homes of friends and family, and at the *masjid*.

She would miss the silent time before dawn.

She shut her eyes tightly and opened her heart as the *Imam* began reciting the hauntingly sweet verses of the Qur´an.

Id al-Fitr

*M*usa's heart leapt as the car climbed uphill. It was the end of *Ramadan* and they were going to see the *Id* moon. A warm breeze rushed into his shirt and puffed it out like a balloon.

"Will we have to fast on *Id*?" he asked.

"No, son," his mother answered. "*Id* is a day of celebration."

They were soon at the top of the hill, overlooking the city. Tiny trees and gray rooftops darkened as the red sun set.

"*Allahu Akbar! Allahu Akbar!*" A tall man faced east and made the call to prayer. During *Ramadan*, the call to prayer (*Adhan*) at sunset also meant that it was time to break the fast. This *Adhan* announced the end of *Ramadan* and the beginning of the celebration of *Id al-Fitr*.

"Look! Look! Is that it?" Fatimah uttered excitedly and pointed her trembling finger upwards.

A hush fell over the crowd, and everybody stopped to look. Sure enough, the thin moon glimmered in the blue-black sky.

"It looks like a finger nail," Musa declared, breathless with happiness.

Dad steered the car into a part of town Musa had never seen before and stopped at a small, wooden house. A dim light flickered on the porch. Musa could smell bread baking.

"Who lives here?" he asked.

"A poor family," Mom explained, as his father went inside. "We must give them something to eat so that Allah will accept our fast. It will also help them to share in the *Id* celebrations."

That night, Musa decorated the house with orange balloons while Fatimah arranged bunches of sweet smelling roses. In the kitchen, Mom poured fruity cake batter into pans. Musa's mouth watered. His eyes burned, as he watched dad crush fresh ginger and chives.

"Turn on the television," Dad instructed him. "The Muslims are airing a program on *Ramadan*."

The program showed Muslims eating the *Suhur*, the early morning meal before dawn, to make them strong for the fast. Families were filmed reading the *Tarawih* prayers, which were prayed every night in the mosques during *Ramadan*.....

"We may or may not live to experience another blessed month of *Ramadan*," Dad said. His eyes glistened with tears. "We can only hope that Allah will accept the fast that we kept."

It was five o'clock on a silent *Id* morning. An icy chill raced down Musa's spine. His heart thumped hard as he burst into the kitchen. The family embraced one another with greetings of the holy day.

Musa and Fatimah exchanged *Id* cards with their parents. Musa's was colorful, and he had written out the greetings himself. Dad read it loudly, "May Allah accept your fast and may He give you a happy *Id*."

"*Id* is a joyous day," he said. "It was a practice of the Prophet Muhammad (peace be upon him) to go out and enjoy this wonderful day."

"Hurry up," Mom urged as they finished praying the *Fajr salah*. "We have to be at the *masjid* by seven o'clock. *Id salah* will be starting at eight."

Musa leapt out of a steamy shower and looked around for his clothes. He hopped about the room wrapped in a towel, but the clothes he had laid out had disappeared. His leg shivered.

"Mom!" he called. "Mom!"

"In here, Musa," his mother answered from the living room.

On the couch, there was a cream-colored suit with a chocolate brown jacket.

Musa swallowed hard. He didn't know what to say. "For me?" he asked.

He ran to hug his parents. From the loving way his mother's eyes were shining, Musa knew that she had sewn it.

"Thank you!" he exclaimed. The fabric was soft under his fingers.

As the car rolled to the *masjid*, Musa recited the *Takbir* softly and reverently, as his father had shown him. *"Allahu Akbar, Allahu Akbar, La Ilaha Illa Allah.* God is the Greatest, God is the Greatest, There is no god but God." The rising sun cleared the morning mist and made the air crisp. They soon halted in front of the green *masjid's* doors.

People greeted one another with joy. Musa went to sit in the front row with his father. The *Imam* began to recite softly. Musa listened carefully and soon caught the words from his Dad. They recit   in praise of the Prophet, his companions, and his family. They asked Allah to bless them all. Musa loved the chanting. It grew louder and louder as more and more people arrived.

The *Id* prayer began at last. The *Imam's* voice poured out rich and sweet like honey. "When we give the charity specific to this blessed holiday, *Zakat al-Fitr*, to the less fortunate people, it purifies us from the mistakes we made while fasting. We could not enjoy the *Id al-Fitr* if our neighbors didn't have food and new clothes."

Friends and relatives, young and old, embraced afterwards. They pressed dollar bills, and gifts into Musa's hands. He felt that he might explode with happiness. But some people looked sad.

"They miss their relatives who are not alive this year," Mom whispered to him. "On *Id* we must remember to pray for those of our relatives and friends who have passed away."

The once empty cars parked outside were now crammed with excited people. One by one, the vehicles rumbled along the city streets. Musa clapped his hands together loudly. They were going to the amusement park!

Laughing families strolled along the boardwalk. The sun danced off the sparkling sapphire lake, and Musa felt like he was flying. Older children rode the noisy roller coaster. The younger ones rode the ferris wheel. They ate cotton candy and popcorn and sipped cold drinks. Sweat trickled down Musa's cheeks. His heart pounded and his head spun. Everyone smiled and joked.

"*Id Mubarak!*" they wished each other: A blessed holiday to you.

When they got home, Fatimah carefully spread the lace table-cloths over the tables, and Musa laid out trays of chocolates and bis-cuits. Mom cooked spicy chicken, bread, and rice.

In the living room, Daddy tossed the scotch tape to Musa.

"Cut this into small pieces for me," he said.

Musa helped him wrap dozens of toys and boxes of candies.

When their guests marched in, the house shone like a jewel.
Dad passed around gifts to the giggling children. Aunt Masuma gave
Fatimah a silk scarf, and Musa got a toy airplane with real windows!
The air was filled with the aroma of delicious food and the hum of
relatives and friends having a good time.

Musa thought about the families who had received *Zakat al-Fitr*.
Because of Allah's kindness, all the poor children were also eating
tasty food and receiving gifts. Thank Allah, they were having a
happy *Id al-Fitr*, too.

When the last guests had gone, Musa's family prayed the night prayer together. Dad said special prayers of thanks and praise.

Then Musa and his father sat down together on the big sofa. They didn't need to say much. They spoke softly about the day and their hopes for the coming years. Musa couldn't wait for *Ramadan* and *Id al-Fitr* to come again. Before he could finish his thought, his eyes fell shut, and he was sound asleep.

47

Id al-Adha

*A*hmad watched as his mother and father packed their things. Ever since he could remember, his parents had spoken about performing the Hajj. Now after years of saving, they were about to fulfill this very important pillar of Islam. Mom's eyes glittered as she packed the medicine bag into the suitcase.

"Hope I didn't leave anything out!" she said, her face was glowing with anticipation.

At the airport, scores of Muslims bade their families farewell. Ahmad felt his throat closing as he hugged his parents. Hot tears streamed down his face as he climbed into Grandpa's car.

"We have to get an animal for the *Id*," Grandpa was saying.

Ahmad stared at him in confusion. "But it's not even *Ramadan*. How can it be *Id* again so soon?"

"Not *Id al-Fitr*," Grandma explained to Ahmad. "*Id al-Adha*. Let me tell you the story...."

"When Prophet Ibrahim's wife Sarah coulnt't have children, he married a noble lady from Egypt name Hajar. They had a son together, and they called him Ismail. Soon after Ismail's birth, however, Allah told Ibrahim to take both Ismail and Hajar to the middle of the blazing hot desert and leave them all alone."

"Did they survive?" Ahamad asked. He felt sorry for the tiny baby Ismail and his mother.

"They did indeed," Grandma answered. "Hajar had faith in Allah. One day, as she was running between the hills of *Safa* and *Marwah* looking for water, Allah showed her a spring called *Zamzam* which still flows today. Allah took good care of the mother and child. And one day, almost nine years later, Ismail, Hajar, and Ibrahim were reunited.

"Prophet Ibrahim was thankful to be back with his son, but in a dream Allah ordered that he sacrifice Ismail."

"Did Prophet Ibrahim tell Ismail about this?" Ahmad wanted to know.

Grandma nodded. "Yes. And Isma'il replied, ´You will find me to be among those who are patient.´

"Well, Ibrahim and Ismail began walking to Mina where the sacrifice would take place. *Shaitan*, the Devil, tried to prevent them from getting to Mina, but on three occasions, Prophet Ibrahim stoned him away, and they continued toward their destination. Today, these spots are marked by three pillars which symbolize the three *Shaitans*."

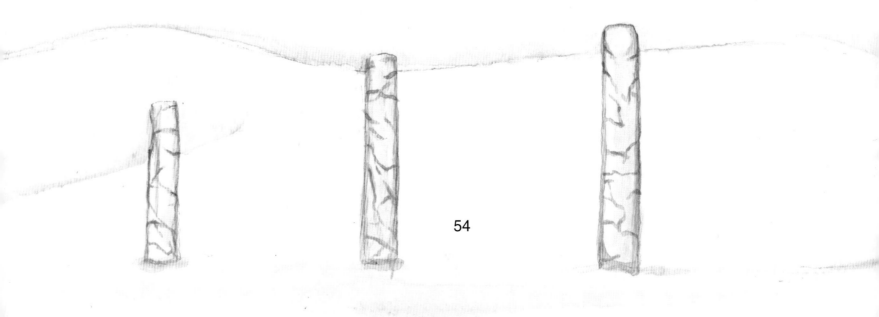

"Did Prophet Ibrahim really kill Ismail when they got to Mina?" Ahmad's heart pounded.

Grandma smiled. "No. The knife stopped. Allah sent a sheep to be sacrificed in Ismail's place. Allah was only testing Prophet Ibrahim's faith!"

Ahmad sighed with relief.

"For this reason, Almighty Allah has ordered that every Muslim who can afford it must slaughter a sheep on the tenth day of the month of *Dhu al-Hijjah* in memory of Prophet Ibrahim and his son Prophet Ismail's obedience," Grandma continued. "Your parents will be making their sacrifice in Mina as part of the Hajj."

The morning of *Id al-Adha* dawned warm and bright. Ahmad pushed off his covers and jumped from his bed. It would be a day brimming with good food, games, and laughter. First, they would head to the *masjid* to pray the *Id* prayer.

On the way to the *masjid*, everyone recited the Takbir: "*Allahu Akbar, Allahu Akbar, La Illaha Illa Allah. Allahu Akbar, wa lillah al-Hamd.*" God is the greatest, God is the Greatest, there is no god but God, and to Him we owe thanks.

The *Imam* first led them in the prayer and then delivered the sermon.

"Allah says that the animal's flesh and blood doesn't reach Him. It is your piety that reaches Him. Our Prophet Muhammad (peace be upon him) has told us that sacrificing animal is a practice of our Prophet Ibrahim and it is a custom in his honor. Every hair on the animal sacrificed will be rewarded for you"

Many people hurried afterwards to perform their sacrifice. Grandpa's car slowed in front of Uncle Mansoor's house.

Ahmad was bursting with excitement. His friends greeted him with wide smiles and shouts. All the children received bright green and pink cellophane bags. Ahmad opened his shyly. The crackling paper revealed a shiny red car, balloons, and candy. The children played and laughed until a film about the Hajj was shown.

Ahmad watched as pilgrims of all races boarded airplanes and ships from their homelands. As they neared Makkah, the men changed into *Ihram*. The *Ihram* was a seamless garment of two pieces of white cloth. One piece was wrapped around the waist; the other draped over the shoulders. The women wore plain dresses. They dressed simply to show they had given up the material world in order to serve God.

The pilgrims went to Mina on the eight of *Dhu al-Hijjah*, to Mount Arafat on the ninth, and then to Muzdalifah where they spent the night. On the day of *Id*, they awoke in Muzdalifah, gathered pebbles, and went to Mina where they stoned one of the pillars representing *Shaitan*. Then they performed the sacrifice. The men shaved their heads and the women trimmed their hair.

Next, the pilgrims put on their regular clothing and went to Makkah. Ahmad gasped when he saw the Holy Ka´bah. It was an enormous cube of bricks, covered with a soft black velvet cloth. The pilgrims circled the Ka´bah seven times. After this *Tawaf*, they kissed he Black Stone and prayed at the tation of Abraham, where rophet Abraham prayed after he ad built the Ka´bah. When the ilgrims marched to and from the ills of *Safa* and *Marwah*, Ahmad emembered Hajar and Ismail.

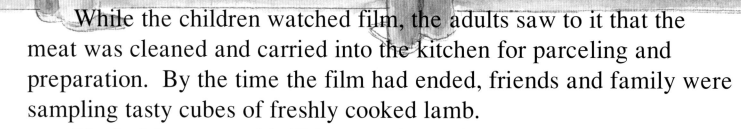

While the children watched film, the adults saw to it that the meat was cleaned and carried into the kitchen for parceling and preparation. By the time the film had ended, friends and family were sampling tasty cubes of freshly cooked lamb.

Uncle Mansoor said, "It's a good practice to give one-third of the meat to needy people, one-third to friends and family, and keep one-third for yourself. A Muslim is supposed to share with others, what-ever God gives him."

Ahmad helped his grandparents with their distribution. They went to the needy homes first. Most of the houses were small and unpainted, and Ahmad was sorry to see barefooted children playing on uneven roads. He followed Grandpa up the stairs to an orphanage. The children grinned happily as Grandpa laid thick slices of steak onto their dinner plates.

At the end of the day, Ahmad could barely stand up. So many friends dropped by to share their meat with them!

"I hope we have room in the freezer," Grandma laughed, as she brought out the trays of chocolates, preserved fruits, and nuts. Ahmad helped serve sodas and coffee to their guests.

As he watched the circles of friends sharing their food and laughter, Ahmad thought about Prophet Ibrahim who was ready to sacrifice the son he loved so much at Allah's command. Even young Ismail was prepared to give up his life for Allah.

Muslims performed the sacrifice and shared with each other to please Allah, Ahmad realized. If they ever had to give up their dearest possessions for Allah's sake, they should be willing, like Prophet Ibrahim was, to do just that.

Glossary

Adhan	Call to prayer
Allahu Akbar!	"God is the Greatest"
Assalamu Alaikum	"Peace be upon you"
Dhu al-Hijjah	The twelfth month of the Islamic calendar; the month of the *Hajj*
Fajr Salah	The dawn prayer
Futur	Breaking the fast at sunset
Hajj	The obligatory pilgrimage to Makkah; one of the five pillars of Islam
Id	Feast; celebration
Id al-Adha	Feast of the sacrifice
Id al-Fitr	Feast of the fast-breaking; this feast marks the end of *Ramadan*.

Id Mubarak	"Blessed *Id*" Muslims say this as an *Id* greeting
Id Salah	Special prayer for *Id* after sunrise
Ihram	Two pieces of white cloth that men wrap around the waist and drape over the shoulders during *Hajj*.
Imam	The leader of a Muslim community
Ka'bah	Cube-shaped building located in the center of the Holy Mousque at Makkah; the point towards which all Muslims pray
Khutbah	Sermon
Lailat al-Qadr	The Night of Power; special blessings are bestowed on the prayerful during this night of *Ramadan* - its blessings are better than a thousand months.
Ma sha Allah!	"Whatever Allah will," Muslims say this when they hear something good or appreciate something

Maghrib Salah	The prayer said at sundown
Masjid	Mosque
Qari' (Muqri)	One who reads the Qur'an beautifully
Ramadan	The holiest month of the year for Muslims; the ninth month of the Islamic calendar; the holy month of fasting
Ramadan Mubarak	"Blessed *Ramadan*" Muslims say this as a *Ramadan* greeting
Shaitan	*Satan*, devil
Suhur	The meal eaten before beginning the fast before dawn
Tarawih	Special *Ramadan* prayers said after the evening prayer
Tawaf	The circling of the *Ka'bah* seven times as an act of worship
Zakat al-Fitr	Charity given to the poor during *Id al-Fitr*